Drama for Students, Volume 25

Project Editor: Ira Mark Milne Rights Acquisition and Management: Beth Beaufore, Jocelyne Green, Jacqueline Key, Kelly Quin, Sue Rudolph Composition: Evi Abou-El-Seoud Manufacturing: Drew Kalasky

Imaging: Lezlie Light

Product Design: Pamela A. E. Galbreath, Jennifer Wahi Content Conversion: Civie Green, Katrina Coach Product Manager: Meggin Condino © 2008 Gale, Cengage Learning

ALL RIGHTS RESERVED. No part of this work covered by the copyright herein may be reproduced, transmitted, stored, or used in any form or by any means graphic, electronic, or mechanical, including but not limited to photocopying, recording, scanning, digitizing, taping, Web distribution, information networks, or information storage and retrieval systems, except as permitted under Section

107 or 108 of the 1976 United States Copyright Act, without the prior written permission of the publisher.

Since this page cannot legibly accommodate all copyright notices, the acknowledgments constitute an extension of the copyright notice.

For product information and technology assistance, contact us at **Gale Customer Support, 1-800-877-4253.**

For permission to use material from this text or product, submit all requests online at **www.cengage.com/permissions.**

Further permissions questions can be emailed to **permissionrequest@cengage.com** While every effort has been made to ensure the reliability of the information presented in this publication, Gale, a part of Cengage Learning, does not guarantee the accuracy of the data contained herein. Gale accepts no payment for listing; and inclusion in the publication of any organization, agency, institution, publication, service, or individual does not imply endorsement of the editors or publisher. Errors brought to the attention of the publisher and verified to the satisfaction of the publisher will be corrected in future editions.

Gale
27500 Drake Rd.
Farmington Hills, MI, 48331-3535

978-0-7876-8121-0
0-7876-8121-0
ISSN 1094-9232

This title is also available as an e-book.
ISBN-13: 978-1-4144-3802-3
ISBN-10: 1-4144-3802-8
Contact your Gale, a part of Cengage Learning sales representative for ordering information.

Printed in the United States of America
1 2 3 4 5 6 7 12 11 10 09 08

The Dumb Waiter

Harold Pinter

1957

Introduction

Harold Pinter's *The Dumb Waiter* (1957) is a two character, one-act play. Set in a claustrophobic basement furnished like a cheap hotel for transients or even a prison cell, it is a study not so much of the two hit men temporarily staying there as they wait for their orders, but of the character of their interaction and of the nature of their condition, and by extension, the nature of the context defining the human condition.

Like cogs in a machine, subject to mysterious directives, bound together but alienated from each other, the hit men follow the orders they are given. They themselves seem to determine nothing. Their entire being is defined by their obedience to invisible, all-powerful, and quietly menacing forces. While the title of the play seems to refer to a small elevator built into the wall, usually used to transport food and trash from one floor in a building to another, Pinter is not referring only to the dumb waiter as a contraption, but to each one of the men as well. Both are waiting; both are dumb; one waits dumbly for the time to carry out an assassination; the other, unknowingly, for his own execution. Indeed, each man is a dumb waiter.

The paramount literary influence on Pinter's play is Samuel Beckett's *Waiting for Godot*, first published in French in 1952 and in Beckett's own English translation in 1954. Essentially, the play is an obscure rendition of two tramps waiting for the arrival of the mysterious Godot, the play seems to be a series of grim vaudeville turns by the two. Nothing really seems to happen except for the meaningless passage of time in a world emptied of meaning in which people live devoid of purpose or power. *Waiting for Godot* was a radically influential and transformative play. Indeed, the influence of *Waiting for Godot* on *The Dumb Waiter* is obvious.

A more recent text of *The Dumb Waiter* can be found in *The Bedford Introduction to Drama*, published in 1989 and edited by Lee A. Jacobus.

Author Biography

Harold Pinter was born to Jewish parents in a working-class neighborhood of East London on October 10, 1930. His father was a tailor. As a child he underwent the terror of being bombed during the Nazi blitzkrieg. The effect was to make an enduring pacifist of him and to embue him with a strong sense of the evil of power and its pervasive menace in human interactions. These issues became the primary concerns of his plays.

In 1948, Pinter entered the Royal Academy of Dramatic Art. But he found the school stultifying and left to join a touring repertory theater that performed extensively throughout England and Ireland. At the same time, he was writing poetry, short stories, and a novel. In 1956, Pinter married Vivien Merchant, an actress, and began writing plays, which sometimes were vehicles for her. Merchant filed for divorce from Pinter in 1975, after he had begun what became a long-standing relationship with the historian Antonia Fraser. Pinter married Fraser after both their divorces were ratified in 1980. With Merchant, Pinter had a son, Daniel, who broke ties with his father after his parents' divorce.

Pinter's first play, *The Room*, was performed in 1957. It flopped. His next play, *The Dumb Waiter*, also written in 1957, was the first in a series of plays, including *The Caretaker* (1959), *The*

Birthday Party (1957), and *The Homecoming* (1964). It was this group of plays that brought Pinter to international prominence and placed him in the same league as dramatists like Samuel Beckett and Eugène Ionesco. In the mid-1950s, these playwrights had begun to produce difficult and disturbing dramas that seemed alien to conventional ideas of theater, focusing particularly on the use of language as a dramatic and a symbolic element. Their plays, moreover, presented worlds that were bleak and fearsome, but also ridiculously meaningless or absurd. This type of drama came to be known as the Theater of the Absurd.

In all, Pinter has written twenty-nine plays. In addition to writing for the theater, Pinter began, in the 1960s, to write original screenplays and adaptations of other writers's work for the movies. He wrote a number of them for the London-based, blacklisted American director, Joseph Losey, and Pinter himself acted in a number of films and on stage.

Although Pinter had refused to serve in the British military in 1948, his plays were seen as bleak representations of reality and not recognized as political statements. In the 1980s, however, Pinter began to be publicly outspoken about political issues. He was ejected from the American embassy in Turkey at a reception in his honor, after he confronted the ambassador from Turkey regarding the torture of prisoners. Pinter has been a resolute critic of the American invasions of Iraq and of the Israeli occupation of Palestinian territories. In his 2005 speech accepting the Nobel Prize, he condemned the United States and the Bush administration for the invasion of Iraq and for its imperial and military activities in general. Pinter did not himself attend the ceremonies in Oslo because of the cancer with which he was diagnosed in 2002; he spoke instead by closed-circuit television. Like so many people living with cancer, Pinter has continued to live a productive life.

Plot Summary

First Encounter

Although *The Dumb Waiter* is a one-act play with no scene divisions, it is unobtrusively divided into a series of encounters between Ben and Gus in what seems to be a dormitory room in the basement of what apparently is or was a restaurant. They seem to be rising from sleep. Gus is tying his shoelaces and Ben, sitting on his bed, is reading the newspaper. Gus walks a few steps and then unties his laces, and takes off his shoes. From within one shoe Gus takes out a flattened, apparently empty box of matches and from the other a flattened pack of cigarettes. Then he puts his shoes back on. As Gus goes through these maneuvers, Ben looks up from his paper and regards him, apparently with disapproval, indicated by a rattling of his newspaper. Once he has put his shoes back on, Gus wanders off the set. Ben follows him with his eyes. Then the sound of a toilet chain being pulled is heard, but it is not followed by the sound of a toilet flushing. When Gus returns, Ben "slams down the paper" and begins talking about a story he has just read in the paper.

An old man who tried to cross a street congested with traffic by crawling under a truck was run over when the truck started to move. The two condemn the inappropriateness of a man of eighty-seven crawling under a truck. When Gus expresses disbelief at the story, twice Ben points out that it must be so because it is written in the paper. The encounter ends when Gus again exits to the lavatory. There is the sound of the chain being pulled but no subsequent sound of the toilet flushing. Gus returns

Second Encounter

Gus tells Ben he wants to ask him a question. Before he can, Ben asks him "What are you doing out there?" Before Gus can answer, Ben shoots another question at him: "What about the tea?" Gus explains he is about to make it. Ben fires back "Well, go on, make it." Instead Gus sits. He begins to describe the crockery. He alludes to someone called "he." "He" has provided "some very nice crockery this time." There is the suggestion of a mysterious superior and that this is not their first "job" for him. What that job is has not been made explicit and never is until the end of the play. Ben asks Gus why he cares about the crockery, ominously adding that he is not going to eat. Gus responds that he has brought a few biscuits. Adding to the sense of foreboding, Ben tells him that he ought to make tea and eat them quickly since there is not much time left.

Media Adaptations

- *The Dumb Waiter*, a 1987 film adaptation of the play, was directed by Robert Altman and stars John Travolta as Ben and Tom Conti as Gus. It was broadcast on television in 1989, and was released on VHS by Prism Entertainment.

Third Encounter

Gus does not go to make tea. He takes out his flattened empty cigarette pack and asks Ben if he has any cigarettes. Ben does not look up from his paper or answer and Gus continues, saying he "hope[s] it won't be a long job, this one," indicating that what they are doing is a routine operation. Ben still makes no response and Gus again says, this time as if remembering he has not yet done so: "Oh, I wanted to ask you something." Instead of responding, or possibly as a response to prevent Gus's question, Ben "slams down" his paper and tells Gus another story from the paper, as if distracting him, about an eight-year-old girl who has been accused of killing a cat. They earnestly speculate if it might have been her brother who did it and blamed her. Ben goes back to his paper and Gus rises.

Fourth Encounter

Gus asks: "What time is he getting in touch?" "He" is presumably their boss. Ben says nothing. Gus repeats the question. Ben responds irritably: "What's the matter with you? It could be any time."

Fifth Encounter

Gus says "I was going to ask you something." Ben says "What?" Gus then asks Ben why the toilet takes so long to flush. The "ballcock" in the toilet is broken, Ben explains. Gus says he had not thought of that. The banality of what they are saying suggests that there is something they are not saying, although what that is remains unclear.

Sixth Encounter

Gus says he has not slept well and complains about the quality of the bed and the lack of a second blanket. His attention is diverted by a picture on the wall of a cricket team. He points it out to Ben, who does not know what he is talking about and asks again: "What about that tea." Gus responds that the members of the team "look a bit old" to him.

Seventh Encounter

Gus remarks that he would not like to live in the room they are in. He wishes there were a window to see outside. Ben asks him what he wants a window for. Gus says that he'd like a view, that it helps pass the time. He complains about his job, that he spends the day enclosed in a room and when he leaves at night, it is dark outside. "You get your holidays, don't you?" Ben retorts. Gus complains that they are only for two weeks. Ben chides him for not appreciating how infrequently they have to work. Ben explains his problem is Gus has no interests. Gus says he does so, but when pressed, cannot name any. Ben mentions several of his and how he is always ready for work. Gus responds by asking Ben if he does not "ever get a bit fed up?" Ben does not know what he is talking about.

Eighth Encounter

Gus is out of cigarettes. The toilet finally flushes. Gus complains some more about working conditions. Remembering their last job, he complains that "He doesn't seem to bother about our comfort much these days." Ben rebukes Gus, telling him to "stop jabbering," but Gus goes on. Ben tells him to make the tea already and that they will not have to wait much longer.

Ninth Encounter

Gus takes out a packet of tea and says that he has been meaning to ask Ben something. Ben says "What the hell is it now?" Gus asks Ben why he stopped "the car that morning, in the middle of a road." Ben answers evasively. "We were too early," he says. The answer does not satisfy Gus. He does not understand how they could be too early since they left after they got a call telling them "to start right away." "Who took the call, me or you?" Ben snaps. Gus admits it was Ben and Ben repeats "We were too early." But Gus can not let it go; "Too early for what?" he says. Ben does not answer. Finally, Gus breaks the silence by supposing the answer that Ben withholds. "You mean someone had to get out before we got in?" Ben remains silent and Gus continues trying to figure things out. He says the sheets on the bed did not look fresh and smelled a little. He complains that he does not want to share his sheets with someone else and remarks that the fact that the sheets are not fresh shows that "things [are] going down the drain" because "we've always had clean sheets laid on up till now." Ben points out that Gus has slept in those sheets all day. Gus concedes that it might be his smell on the sheets and perhaps he does not know what he himself smells like.

Tenth Encounter

Ben looks at the newspaper. Finally, he interrupts his silence, exclaiming "Kaw!" about something he has just read. Gus asks what town they are in? He says he has forgotten. Ben tells him Birmingham. Gus suggests that they can go to watch the city's soccer team play. Ben tells him that they are playing away, that there is no time, anyhow. Gus points out that "in the past," they stayed over to watch a game. Ben's response is ominous: "Things have tightened up, mate." Gus says that they have never been to Tottenham or "done a job" there, Ben contradicts him. Gus says that he would remember Tottenham. Ben says "Don't make me laugh, will you?" Gus wonders when "he" is going to get in touch with them. Ben does not respond. Gus shifts the subject back to soccer. They argue about which team is playing where, Ben contradicting whatever Gus says.

Eleventh Encounter

A new force enters the play. "An envelope slides under the door." Gus notices it and points it out to Ben. Ben asks what it is. Gus says he does not know. Ben tells him to pick it up. Gus approaches it slowly and picks it up. Ben continues to direct him. Gus opens it. There are matches inside. He hands Ben the envelope. There is no note included. Ben orders Gus to open the door to see if he can catch whoever slipped the envelope under it. Gus gets his gun, opens the door, but no one is there. Gus puts his gun back under his pillow.

Twelfth Encounter

Gus looks at the matches, comments that they will come in handy, and he and Ben go back and forth about how useful the matches are, how Gus is always running out of matches, and finally, Gus says "I can light the kettle now." He does not move to do that, however, and they talk a little more about the matches until Ben slaps Gus's hand as Gus cleans his ear with one of the matches, telling him not to waste them but to go and "light it." Gus has just said he "can light the kettle now," but he does not know what Ben is referring to. They bandy words back and forth until it is clear that Ben is telling him to make tea. Before he begins to, Gus and Ben argue whether properly speaking one says "light the kettle" or "light the gas." Ben says "Light the Kettle." Gus says, "You mean the gas," even though he himself had just used the expression "light the kettle." Ben responds "What do you mean, I mean the gas," ominously as his eyes, according to the stage directions, narrow. The inane but sinister argument continues for a good twenty lines with Ben attacking and Gus defending himself until a moment of real and senseless violence erupts when Ben grabs Gus "with two hands by the throat, at arm's length," and yells "THE KETTLE, YOU FOOL!" Gus capitulates, saying "All right, all right," but does nothing. Ben asks him what he is waiting for. Gus says he wants to see if the matches light. He strikes one on the box; it does not. He tosses the matches under the bed and retrieves them as Ben stares at him. He strikes a match on his shoe and it lights. Fed up, Ben says "Put on the bloody kettle, for Christ's sake," realizing it is an expression he had derided in the foregoing argument. Gus goes out and then returns, saying "It's going." When Ben says "What?" Gus says "The stove," using the word "stove" instead of "kettle" or "gas."

Thirteenth Encounter

The question Gus has been trying to ask Ben begins to emerge when Gus muses "I wonder who it'll be tonight." He clears his throat and says "I've been wanting to ask you something." Ben expresses annoyance that Gus is "always asking [him] questions." Ben then asks Gus why he is sitting on his [Ben's] bed. He says Gus never used to ask "so many damn questions." He asks him "what's the matter with you?" Gus tries to defend himself by saying—before he even gets to ask the question—"No, I was just wondering." Ben tells him to "stop wondering," to do his job and "shut up." But Gus is not thwarted. He says that was what he was wondering about. Ben responds as if he does not know what Gus is talking about. Gus asks hesitantly "who it's going to be tonight?" Ben refuses to answer, seeming not to know what Gus is talking about, throwing questions like "Who what's going to be?" and "Are you feeling alright?" back at him. And Ben tells him again, "Go and make the tea." Nothing is said, but something sinister is evident.

Fourteenth Encounter

Ben is alone as Gus is offstage making tea. He takes his revolver out from under his pillow and makes sure it is loaded. Inspecting the weapon while Gus is offstage, suggests that he knows something Gus does not about how the gun will be used.

Gus reenters, not yet having made tea because there is no gas and he does not have a shilling to drop in the gas meter, nor does Ben. Ben says they will have to wait for Wilson for the shilling. But he might not come; "he might just send a message." Wilson never does appear. Waiting for Wilson satirizes the main conceit of Samuel Beckett's *Waiting for Godot*. Ben tells Gus he just might have to wait for his tea until afterwards. As Gus complains that he likes to have his tea beforehand, Ben "holds the revolver up to the light and polishes it," telling Gus "you'd better get ready."

Gus is becoming irritable. He grumbles about the fact that Wilson has not provided gas. When he says that the room they are staying in is Wilson's "place," Ben challenges him, but Gus insists it is. As he speaks he begins to wonder about the other jobs they have done for Wilson, how "nobody ever hears a thing," how Wilson does not always show up at all, how difficult he finds it to talk to him. Ben tells him to be quiet, but Gus persists, wondering "about the last one." Ben acts as if he does not know what Gus is talking about, and Gus says it is about "that girl."

Fifteenth Encounter

Ben ignores what Gus has just said and angrily goes back to reading the newspaper. Gus, who had been rather compliant, has become frustrated and impatient. He has not had his tea, after all. He asks "How many times have you read that paper?" In anger "Ben slams the paper down," asks Gus what he means, threatens to box him in the ear if he does not watch out, accuses him of taking liberties, and warns him, when Gus tries to explain, to "get on with it, that's all." But Gus has begun to wonder about his past jobs and cannot stop talking. He reverts to the subject of the girl. From what he says, it appears that they killed her. Gus is disturbed, not because they killed her, but because of the messiness involved and wonders who cleans up after them. Ben calls him a fool.

Sixteenth Encounter

They hear a noise inside the wall between the beds and notice that a dumb waiter is built into the wall. Inside the dumb waiter is a note appearing to be an order for food. It reads "Two braised steak and chips. Two sago puddings. Two teas without sugar." Gus comments on the tea, not having been able to have any himself and now apparently being directed to make some for others. Gus is puzzled at the order, but Ben says that the place must have been a café, that it has "change[d] hands," and that where they are had been a kitchen. Gus wonders who owns the place now. "Well, that all depends,"

Ben says. He is interrupted by the clatter of the dumb waiter. This time the piece of paper reads "Soup of the day. Liver and onions. Jam tart." Do these words signify actual food items as they usually do, or are they codes, perhaps informing Ben about a decision higher-ups have made with regard to the job? The interpretative limits for this text seem to be flexible. Some silent business follows. Ben looks into the dumb waiter but not up the shaft. Gus, behind him, puts his hand on Ben's shoulder and Ben throws it off. Gus then looks into the dumb waiter and *up* the shaft. This gesture alarms Ben who pushes Gus away from the dumb waiter, tosses his gun onto the bed and tells Gus that they had better "send something up." Gus agrees and when he goes to shout something up the dumb waiter, Ben stops him. They go through a bag of food Gus has with him, noting the items. Ben suggests they send the packet of tea; Gus objects, pointing out it is all the tea they have. Ben reminds him it is useless since they can not turn on the gas. Gus says "Maybe they can send us down" a coin for the gas meter. Ben ignores him and asks what else Gus has in his bag and Gus takes out a sugared pastry called an Eccles cake. Ben scolds Gus for never having told him he had brought one and he scolds him as well for only bringing one and none for him. He adds that they can not "send up" just one Eccles cake but does not answer when Gus asks "Why not?" Instead he tells Gus to get a plate. Gus asks if he cannot keep the cake since "they don't know we've got it." But Ben tells him he can not keep it. Then Ben finds a bag of potato chips in

Gus's bag and the same routine is repeated as Ben scolds Gus, telling him he is "playing a dirty game," and "I'll remember this," presumably not just for failing to declare all his food, but for the insubordination that this reflects. Once they have piled up the food they have gathered on a plate and are about to put it in the dumb waiter, before they can, the dumb waiter goes up empty. Ben tells Gus it is his fault for "playing about," that they will have to wait until it comes down again. Ben puts the plate on the bed, puts on his shoulder holster and begins to knot his tie. He tells Gus he ought to get ready.

Seventeenth Encounter

Gus puts on his tie and shoulder holster. He wonders how their room can be a café since the gas stove has only three rings, not allowing for much cooking. Ben answers dryly: "That's why the service is slow." Gus keeps up his inconsequential chatter and Ben does not answer him. The dumb waiter returns. Gus retrieves a note demanding more dishes, the redundantly named "Macaroni Pastitsio" and the exotic "Ormitha Macarounada." He puts the plate of their snacks on the dumb waiter and shouts its contents into the shaft. The dumb waiter goes up and Ben reprimands Gus for having yelled because "it isn't done." He then tells him to get dressed because "It'll be any minute now."

Eighteenth Encounter

Gus continues complaining about the "place," especially about the lack of tea and biscuits. Ben tells him that eating "makes you lazy" and that Gus is getting lazy. He asks Gus if he has checked his gun and notes that he never polishes it. "Gus rubs his revolver on the sheet." Ben fixes his tie in preparation for the job. Gus continues his chatter. He wonders about the cook and if there is another kitchen and if there are more gas stoves. Ben assures him, with dry condescension, that there are. He asks Gus if he knows "what it takes to make an Ormitha Macarounada." Gus does not. Ben begins to tell him, but cuts himself short before he says anything and tells Gus to be quiet.

Gus puts his revolver in its holster and continues to complain. He wants to get out of the place. He wonders why "he" has not gotten in touch with them yet. He says that he and Ben have always done "reliable" work. He hopes their job is easy. He has a bad headache. The dumb waiter descends again with more food orders and the packet of tea they had sent up. They can not fill the orders and Ben says "urgently" that they "better tell them" so. As he is about to write a note, he discovers a speaking tube he had not seen, in the wall, beside the dumb waiter. Gus first speaks into the tube after they figure out how it works and says "The larder's bare!" Ben takes the tube from him and politely repeats that there is no more food. Someone on the other end seems to be complaining about the inadequacy of each of the items they have sent up. The conversation ends as Ben reports that the voice instructed him to "light the kettle!" suggesting the earlier argument about the correct idiom, but Gus points out "there's no gas." He is annoyed at being instructed to make tea for others when there is none for him. Ben says nothing. Noticing how bad Ben looks, Gus says that he could use an "Alka-Seltzer" himself. Ben says that the time is near.

Nineteenth Encounter

Gus complains that he does not like having to do the job while he is hungry. Ben silences him, saying he must give him his instructions. Gus does not know why since they always do the same thing. Ben repeats "Let me give you your instructions." He states them; Gus repeats them. They never mention the actual deed of killing, only all their moves preceding that. When they finish, Gus "shivers," exits, and the sound of the toilet chain pulled in the lavatory is heard.

Twentieth Encounter

Gus reenters; he is troubled and thoughtful. Why, he asks Ben, did "he" send them matches when "he knew there was no gas." Ben does not answer. Gus repeats the question twice. Ben answers he does not know what Gus is talking about. Gus continues: "Who is it upstairs?" Ben evades the question, commanding Gus to be silent. Gus persists. Ben commands him to "Shut up!" Ben hits him twice on the shoulder "viciously." That does not stop Gus. Nearly hysterical, he cries out "What's he doing it for? We've been through our tests.... What's he playing these games for?" As he is ranting, the dumb waiter returns. Gus "seizes" the note, which is an order for "Scampi." He crumples the note and frantically yells through the tube: "WE'VE GOT NOTHING LEFT! NOTHING! DO YOU UNDERSTAND?" Ben pushes him away, calls him a maniac, screams "That's enough," and replaces the speaking tube.

The dumb waiter ascends, Gus and Ben look each other in the eye. Gus sits on his bed. Ben starts to read the paper, throws it down, exclaims "Kaw!" as he had earlier when other stories caught his attention, and says "Have you ever heard such a thing?" without saying what he is reading. The two of them comment incredulously about the unrecounted story.

Gus leaves, he says, to get a glass of water. The whistle of the speaking tube blows. Ben answers and is told it is time and that the mark will be coming in right away. Ben hangs up the tube, calls to Gus twice, combs his hair, and is ready. The toilet is heard to flush. Gus stumbles in through the door stripped of his jacket, vest, tie, holster, and revolver. He looks at Ben. In silence, "they stare at each other."

Characters

Ben

Ben is one of the two men waiting in a basement to carry out what appears to be a hired killing. He is the one in charge of the operation. He is rather quiet and does not question his assignments or complain about his working conditions. He spends the time waiting reading the newspaper and is fascinated by odd human interest stories usually involving strange twists of violence, like an old man being killed ducking under a truck or some youngsters killing a cat. He is often evasive when he speaks. He tells his partner as little as possible about their assignment and often responds to his questions by saying he does not know what he is talking about. His attitude towards his superiors is deferential. He believes in their authority and, in a limited way, has authority himself. After his partner, Gus, shouts into a speaking tube, Ben apologizes to whoever is on the other end. He is capable of violence and lunges at Gus when he cannot contain his rage at Gus's undisciplined behavior. He gives orders to Gus without feeling the need to explain himself. He often demeans Gus and treats him with condescension and disdain. Ben insists that his way of speaking or doing things is the correct way. If the play is seen as the symbolic representation of mankind's powerlessness in the face of a cruel God or cruel fate, Ben can be seen as the agent of that cruelty. If viewed from a psychological standpoint, Ben is tormented by his very role as an agent of torment.

The Dumb Waiter

The dumb waiter—commonly found in a house built for servants—is a small elevator to carry things between floors. Although conventionally a prop, the dumb waiter can be seen as a kind of mechanical character in the play. It is used to convey orders to the two men in the basement from an unidentified character upstairs. The orders it carries seem to be orders for food, but the mysterious context in which they arrive can make them seem like codes or representations of demands made on mankind by higher forces, demands that seem unreasonable or impossible to fulfill either because of mankind's inadequacy or the exotic quality of the demand. Although only a mechanical object, in the play the dumb waiter is given almost metaphysical power. It can signify the confusion in communication that people often experience in their interactions. It can also be seen as the imperfect channel of communication between mankind and an unseen deity or incomprehensible fate.

Gus

Gus is talkative, inquisitive, and even resentful of his superiors. Whereas Ben spends much of the time they are waiting sitting on his bed reading the newspaper, Gus is often in motion, taking off and putting on his shoes, going to the toilet, fooling with matches, or looking at the crockery. He knows nothing about the job they are going to do, and, despite its apparently grim nature, his chief concern is to have his tea. When he is unable to have tea, it frustrates him greatly. Gus also tries to withhold some of his food when Ben suggests they send it upstairs in an attempt to meet the demands of the person or people sending down orders. His food becomes a sacrificial object to send up, foreshadowing Gus himself as a sacrificial object. But the sacrifice seems meaningless. Gus complains about how he and Ben are treated by the man they are working for. He is bored, objects to the smell of their bed sheets or the lack of a window in the room. Whereas Ben is an executioner, Gus is a victim. At the end of the play, it appears that he is the person they have been assigned to kill. Unlike Ben, Gus has doubts about what they are doing and is full of troubled questions about their situation. He is inefficient and slow in obedience. He is not really tough but rather desperately childlike and confused. He displays a rebellious nature, raging against an authority that is incomprehensible to him. If the play is read as a symbolic representation of mankind's predicament in relation to God or fate, Gus represents the desperation people can feel who sense themselves abandoned in a world without meaning or a loving God. In terms of the play's structure, it is Gus who propels the action by his questions, complaints and outbursts.

The Room

The room Ben and Gus wait in is entirely nondescript except for its two beds and two doors, one on the left, one on the right. It has no windows but it can communicate to a limited world outside, to a bathroom through the doors, and to the upstairs through the dumb waiter and a speaking tube. It is possible to think of the room as signifying a place of testing for both Ben and Gus. Indeed, Gus cries out that they have already been tested and demands to know why they are being tested again. In Jean-Paul Sartre's one-act play, *No Exit* (1944), hell is represented by three people confined to a single room for eternity. In *The Dumb Waiter*, the room Ben and Gus occupy can be thought of as a kind of purgatory through which they are passing, but a purgatory that leads them not to Heaven but to a Hell of coldly uncaring meaninglessness.

Wilson

Wilson is not an on-stage character in *The Dumb Waiter* but is mentioned by Ben and Gus as the man they are working for and who may or may not appear. He is often only referred to as "he," reinforcing his shadowy nature and mysterious presence. Nothing is really known about him. Perhaps he is the person upstairs sending orders down on the dumb waiter. Perhaps it is someone else. It is not clear if Ben and Gus work for one man or for an amorphous organization. Perhaps they, as well as the audience, do not know. As a character who never appears, Wilson is similar to Godot, in Samuel Beckett's *Waiting for Godot*, a play in which two characters interact in a barren landscape as they wait for the mysterious Godot to appear. Why they are waiting and what he will bring them are not revealed. Wilson, like Godot, can be thought of as representing a God who is himself hidden and whose purposes are hidden, a god who makes all of us into dumb waiters—people waiting stupidly or quietly for something and ultimately only finding death.

Themes

Alienation

While the word alienation is never mentioned in *The Dumb Waiter*, the atmosphere of the play reeks of it. Ben and Gus, long-time partners who have worked closely together, are isolated from each other. Their overt conversation is composed of empty exchanges about articles in the newspaper. The conversation that goes on beneath the surface, which is expressed through their attitude towards each other, shows distance and evasion governing their intercourse. The work they do is also representative of a fundamental alienation in their world. They have no say in where they go or what they do. They seem unsure about the forces for whom they work or exactly what is wanted of them by their superiors, as all the business with the orders coming on the dumb waiter suggests. In addition the work they do, killing people, is a pure example of alienation.

Avoidance

Pinter is often discussed as a playwright whose concern is to show the difficulties or the failures in communication that people experience. More pointedly, in *The Dumb Waiter*, Pinter seems to be showing how people use words to avoid communicating. In *The Dumb Waiter* he seems to be exploring the rhetoric of evasion. Ben repeatedly uses the newspaper to give him things to talk to Gus about, and the two of them become entangled passionately in discussions and arguments about the most trivial things from weird news items such as which soccer team was playing where. Meanwhile, Ben particularly avoids any real contact or conversation with Gus, who does strive for it. Ben's evasion is necessary considering what seems to be the underlying plot of the play, that he is about to kill Gus at a moment that will be determined for him.

Betrayal

The suggestion of betrayal is implicit in *The Dumb Waiter*. No overt reason for the tension between Ben and Gus is ever presented, but there are suggestions that Ben, who is Gus's partner and superior, seems to know something that he is withholding from Gus. What was he thinking about when he stopped their car as he was driving to the job while Gus was asleep in the seat next to him? Gus wants to know, but Ben does not say. Similarly, Ben warns Gus several times throughout the play that he is getting lazy and that his attitude towards his work and his superiors is poor. In their last confrontation, as Gus stumbles disarmed into the room and Ben faces him with a gun, while ambiguity still lingers regarding Ben's previous knowledge that it is Gus whom he was hired to kill, it seems likely that Ben did know it. The ambiguity of the last moments leaves open the question of whether he will complete his betrayal of his partner or, as it were, betray his superiors. Ironically, from the point of view of those superiors who have ordered Gus's extermination, Gus himself is the one having betrayed them by his questioning, resentful, and rebellious attitude. By ordering Ben to kill Gus they are, in addition, forcing him to betray himself, hence his irritability towards Gus. Ben must purge himself of any fellow feeling for Gus.

Obedience and Resistance

The work that Ben and Gus do requires unquestioning obedience to the to forces that direct them but of which they are only peripherally aware. As hired killers, they are expected to surrender moral judgment, human compassion, awareness of the humanity of the Other and replace those traits with unstinting, unquestioning obedience. Their obedience is demanded in seemingly lesser matters, too, as their anxiety to fulfill the food orders that come via the dumb waiter show. The apparent fault that puts Gus in danger is the beginning of curiosity, questioning, and self-assertion, feeble as it is, that he displays. Obedience always faces a threat from the opposite that it generates, which is resistance. The traits Gus shows are threats to obedience. Ben, on the other hand, shows himself, until the end of the play, to be perfectly obedient. It is not clear whether his obedience will continue or if something else in him will prevail. It is reasonable to assume that Ben's extreme irritation with Gus throughout the play is a result of a conflict within himself between his obedience to his masters and some sort of fellow-feeling towards his partner, a feeling he must stifle.

Topics for Further Study

- Pinter's early plays, like *The Dumb Waiter*, often called "comedies of menace," reflect the spirit of the 1950s, a decade characterized by a number of generalized anxieties about nuclear war, gang violence, economic repression, political witch hunts, and nervous breakdowns. Choose any one of these areas to research. Write an essay on your findings, introducing and exploring the issue, and setting it in historical, political, economic, and cultural contexts. Using your paper as a basis, introduce and explain the issue to your class.

- In addition to *The Dumb Waiter*, read Pinter's plays *The Room*, *The Caretaker*, and *The Homecoming*. Write an essay exploring the ways these plays resemble and differ from each other in terms of plot, characters, themes, dramatic construction, and tone.

- With one other member of your class, perform *The Dumb Waiter* or a selection from it for your class. Prepare a working script of the play in which you note the interpretive choices you have made, such as the way you choose to deliver the lines or the way you move on stage. Then explain why you have made those choices.

- The characters in *The Dumb Waiter* use speech as a way of avoiding communication. Write a story in which the characters speak with each other, interact, and do things together but never really say what is on their minds. Or, describe a situation in which you avoided saying what you wanted to say and another situation where you spoke to cover up what you meant. How is such speech different (or not different) from lying?

- Write a sequel to *The Dumb Waiter*. What can happen next? If you think that there is not a possible sequel to *The Dumb Waiter*, despite its open ending, write an essay discussing why you feel this way. Be sure to cite examples from the play in support of your argument.

- Lead a class debate based on this question: Is there a hero and a villain in *The Dumb Waiter*? If so, who is the hero, and who is the villain? Why? If not, why not?

Style

Interactions Presented as Encounters

The Dumb Waiter is a one-act play performed without interruption. Pinter achieves a sense of structure by setting up a series of encounters between the two characters. These encounters flow one into the next but each one is also complete in itself within the context of the play, the way a scene is. The encounters establish a pattern in the relationship between Ben and Gus and they serve to define the characteristics of each. The encounters have the shape of old vaudeville routines and they mix the comic interaction and timing of those kinds of routines with an underlying quality of menace that is conveyed by the intensity of each character's participation in those routines. The climax of the play, when Ben repeatedly punches Gus in the shoulder, transforms slapstick into anxious rage. The final moments of the play, a second climax, is only a nonverbal encounter in which the ambiguity of the relationship between Ben and Gus hovers unresolved over the play and over the audience, as if removed from the play and given to the audience as a choice. The choice is between the kind of alienated, evasive relationships presented in the play, the kind that must terminate in betrayals of both oneself and other people, or relationships that begin to realize a shared essential something that can connect people to each other. The final encounter in *The Dumb Waiter*, then, is not the climactic encounter between Ben and Gus but an encounter between the play itself and its audience.

Pauses

The word "pause" appears nearly two dozen times as a stage direction in *The Dumb Waiter*, the word "silence" some half a dozen times, and a notation that the two characters stare at each other without saying anything appears frequently, too. The play ends, in fact, with the direction that there is a long silence in which the characters stare at each other. If the spoken words in *The Dumb Waiter* are essential tools of evasion and signify alienation, the pauses, silences, and moments when Ben and Gus stare at each other signify, without being conveyed by verbal props, the essential but buried matter of the play—the mysterious connection and the incipient betrayal that constitutes the relationship between the two characters and the action of the drama. What is hidden by talk is revealed, even if only darkly, by silences. The anxiety, confusion, conflict, and tension governing the interactions between Ben and Gus provoke a sense of some indefinably menacing danger hovering about and defining the texture of the world they inhabit.

Historical Context

The Cold War

The sense of indefinable menace and of insecurity that permeates *The Dumb Waiter* reflects the Zeitgeist, or spirit of the time, that pervaded the 1950s because of the Cold War. The Cold War was a conflict between the United States and the Soviet Union, now Russia, and a group of smaller countries, for political, military, and economic control of the globe. In its most menacing form, the Cold War consisted of an arms race between the two super powers, as they were called, to build the most daunting weaponry, particularly in the form of nuclear bombs. The Soviet Union and the United States had been allies against Nazi Germany, Fascist Italy, and Imperial Japan during World War II from 1939-1945. After the war, they slowly became foes, partly because of different political structures.

The war against Japan ended when Harry Truman, then President of the United States, ordered the dropping of atomic bombs on the Japanese cities of Hiroshima, on August 6, 1945, and Nagasaki, on August 9, 1945. In addition to destroying these two Japanese cities, the dropping of the atomic bombs announced to the world, and especially to the Soviet Union's dictator, Joseph Stalin, that the United States was a power to fear.

Stalin, after the war, had imperial designs on many of the countries of Europe and indeed managed to subordinate many Eastern European countries to the Soviet Union. In response to the American bombs, the Russians also built nuclear weapons, and each country established bases from which they pointed their weapons at the other country's major cities. This policy of Mutually Assured Destruction both kept the balance of power between the two super states and caused a general malaise among most of the people, as well as resistance in some. There were general, compulsory shelter drills that people, including school children, were forced to participate in. Some, like the philosopher/mathematician Bertram Russell in Britain, protested the building, testing, and deploying of nuclear weapons. The menacing sense of looming danger pervasive in *The Dumb Waiter* reflects this cultural condition.

Gangster Movies

The models for the two hit men, Ben and Gus, are the gangsters in the films Hollywood turned out in the 1940s and 1950s where gangsters were played as suave and debonair, yet disturbing and menacing, characters by actors like Humphrey Bogart, Edward G. Robinson, Farley Granger, George Raft, Yul Brynner, Dan Duryea, and James Cagney. They were often odd mixtures of brutality and delicacy, of charm and cruelty, of bravado and cowardice. They were suave and crude, attractive and repellent, narcissistic poseurs without a strong center. Ben tries to maintain an air of cool detachment, reading the paper, stoically doing his job. He makes sure to fix his tie and comb his hair before he goes into action. Not only does Pinter model his thugs on the hero-gangsters of these movies, but the characters themselves, especially Ben, seem to be deliberately modeling themselves on the movie images.

The Holocaust

Between 1933 and 1945, the Nazi German government rounded up some ten million people, among them Jews, Gypsies, homosexuals, and communists, and incarcerated and systematically exterminated them. Without warning, a knock could come at the door and a whole family, or whole towns, could be taken, in minutes, to places known as death camps. The sense of dread this introduced into the world's psyche is reflected in *The Dumb Waiter*.

The Organization Man

The idea of the organization man, a man who worked for, and conformed to, the dictates of a large corporation—which became the source not only of his income but the arbiter of everything about the way he lived his life, raised his family, and comported himself—strongly influenced the mainstream culture of the 1950s. The critical response to that culture by writers and artists trying to make sense of or reform, reshape, and, from their point of view, reinvigorate that culture, became a powerful counter-cultural movement in this decade and the decade that followed. Ben and Gus can be seen as serious parodies of those men and the organization they work for is a shadowy representation of those corporate entities.

Compare & Contrast

- **1950s:** An air of fear and menace taints many human interactions and ways of thinking because of the Cold War, which pits countries like Great Britain and the United States on one side against the Soviet Union on the other. Each side has a cause for anxiety because each has the capability to engage in nuclear warfare.

    Today: An air of fear and menace taints many human interactions and ways of thinking because of the "War on Terror," which pits western governments like the United States and Great Britain against several Middle Eastern governments and religious factions who believe themselves to be waging a holy war and who stage terrorist attacks around the world.

- **1950s:** "Organization men" working for large corporations shape their lives to conform to the rules set down by their employers. They seem to be cogs in a great machine rather than spontaneous individuals.

Today: In the global economy, workers are treated like interchangeable parts of a great machine. Rather than becoming integral parts of a corporation which they serve and which offers them a secure, lifelong career, people experience uncertainty in their jobs and face the possibility of layoffs and corporate downsizing.

- **1950s:** People are distracted from their anxieties and from independent and organized opposition, in Western Europe and the United States, by public relations, entertainment, sports, and advertising.

Today: People are distracted from their anxieties and from independent and organized opposition, in Western Europe and the United States by public relations, entertainment, sports, advertising, and technological gadgetry.

The Theater of the Absurd

Theater of the Absurd refers to a kind of play written during the 1940s, 1950s, and 1960s, primarily in Europe, and especially in France. Playwrights like Albert Camus, Jean Genet, Jean-Paul Sartre, Samuel Beckett, Fernando Arabal, Edward Albee, Harold Pinter, and Eugèene Ionesco wrote dramas that reflected their vision of a world that had lost meaning and purpose. Camus, in *The Myth of Sysiphus* used the term "the absurd" to characterize a philosophy of existence that saw no meaning in the universe and made each individual responsible for the creation of meaning and purpose despite the emptiness of existence. The term "Theater of the Absurd" was invented by the theater critic Martin Esslin in 1962 when he wrote a book of that name exploring the work of these playwrights.

Vaudeville

Pinter's dialogue is often reminiscent of the kind of routines that were perfected in vaudeville by teams of comedians, one being a straight man and the other bouncing off him to deliver the laugh lines. The routines usually worked due to the confusion that existed between the two because each had a different frame of reference from his partner when he spoke. By the 1950s, vaudeville in theaters was pretty much a thing of the past, replaced by movies and, especially, by television. But television, in the 1950s, did not destroy vaudeville. It simply caused it to relocate, leaving the grand movie palaces and lodging on the small home screen. The routines in *The Dumb Waiter* often are reminiscent of the kind of routines performed by the great vaudeville acts like (George) Burns and (Gracie) Allen or Jack Benny—a master of the frozen pause and silent, sidelong glance—and one of his several straightmen, or especially of (Bud) Abbott and (Lou) Costello. All these were popular television performers in the 1950s. One of Abbott and Costello's most famous routines, "Who's on First," seems particularly relevant to *The Dumb Waiter* because of the rhythm of its banter and because of the way it highlights the frustrations of non-communication, especially when words become devoid of meaning.

Critical Overview

"The drama of Harold Pinter," Katherine H. Burkman wrote in *The Dramatic World of Harold Pinter: Its Basis in Ritual*, "evolves in an atmosphere of mystery." Burkman continues: "While the surfaces of life are realistically detailed, the patterns below the surface are as obscure as the motives of the characters." The mysterious quality that informs *The Dumb Waiter* is specifically a function of Pinter's strategy of removing any information that can set the action of the play or the attitudes of its characters in context. The audience knows nothing about them but what they say in the course of their conversations with each other, which is little indeed. This scarcity of information has been the focus of much critical discussion. R. A. Buck, writing in the *Explicator*, cites Thomas F. Van Laan's observation that readers and critics often fill in "what [Pinter] has supposedly neglected to record." Buck then states that "by 'filling in' an absurdist play, we risk losing sight of the precise language of the text and thus its performing function." Buck proceeds to argue that this "has happened to such an extent in Pinter criticism that discussions of the ending of *The Dumb Waiter* have neglected to emphasize the power of the linguistic ambiguity in the last lines of the play." While he attempts to avoid what he considers an interpretive error by conducting a close reading of the closing stage directions of the play, Buck, too, fills in what might be happening but is not textually indicated, suggesting the possibility that Gus enters through the door on the left and someone else, unspecified, enters as the door on the right is thrown open. Indeed, it is, according to Van Laan, inevitable that readers help construct the events of the play, just because so much is omitted and much of what is included in *The Dumb Waiter* seems to be functioning to avoid rather than to reveal what has happened, what is happening, and what will happen.

Despite the room for filling in that exists in *The Dumb Waiter*, most critics actually do agree on the essentials of the play. "Two men ... are on assignment and wait for the specific details in a basement room," James R. Hollis comments in *Harold Pinter: The Poetics of Silence*. After a straightforward summary of what occurs on the surface, Hollis suggests that it is possible to "allegorize *The Dumb Waiter*," to read the play symbolically. The very bareness of the play invites this; the play is, after all, an attempt to find meaning where meaning as it is generally experienced is absent. Hollis suggests that "the hierarchical power upstairs could be identified as a deity…. The little creatures scurry about on their terrestrial plane and try to guess what [he] wants." But Hollis rejects this sort of reading as unnecessary, as do most of Pinter's critics. Rather than theological readings, most critics take a more down to earth tack. Hollis considers that what is represented in *The Dumb Waiter* is "man's suspicion that there is a power that is not so much malevolent as detached and unconcerned." This interpretation stands without identifying that power as supernatural or, for example, corporate or governmental. Hollis sees Gus and Ben as alternative possible responses to the mystery of such a dominant power: one submits and one rebels. Arnold P. Hinchliffe, writing in *Harold Pinter*, presents a more sociological reading, quoting the Yugoslavian critic Istvan Sinko: "When the functionary begins to reflect on the meaning of his job, he must die." Hinchliffe himself refuses to be as specific, concluding a survey of critical responses to *The Dumb Waiter* by observing that "Pinter's exploration of the lower depths has an unmistakable, if indefinable, relevance to life as we live it."

What Do I Read Next?

- Pinter's play *Betrayal* (1978) was made into a film with Ben Kingsley and Jeremy Irons in 1983. It portrays the story of a long adulterous affair in reverse chronological order. As in *The Dumb Waiter*, Pinter works with themes of trust and betrayal in a situation where one character knows of another's disadvantage while the other does not.

- *Dutchman* (1964) is a one-act play by Amiri Baraka, who was then writing under his birth name of LeRoi Jones. The play was made into a film in 1967. The play concerns the menacing and finally violent encounter between a young black man and a young white woman who are alone together in a subway car. As in *The Dumb Waiter*, the play is set in a confined space and the characters have no means of escape.

- Israel Horovitz's play *The Indian Wants the Bronx* opened in 1968 with Al Pacino in the leading role of a street punk who terrorizes an East Indian visitor to New York City who has stopped to ask him for directions. As in *The Dumb Waiter*, the play uses a seemingly everyday situation and transforms it into a life and death confrontation.

- *Our Lady of the Flowers*, by the French poet, novelist, homosexual, and thief, Jean Genet, was written in prison and first appeared in French in 1943. It was published in an English translation by Bernard Fretchman in 1963. It tells the story of a French drag queen and his pimp lover, who betrays him as an act of love. As Pinter does in *The Dumb Waiter*, Genet explores the ambiguity of a relationship between two men, one of whom seems to be dominant and the other submissive. Genet's language, unlike Pinter's minimalism, is richly ornate.

- Samuel Beckett's *Waiting for Godot* was first performed in its original French in 1952 in Paris and in 1955 in London in an English translation made by Beckett himself. It concerns two tramps waiting, for some unspecified reason, in a kind of no man's land for someone, or something, named Godot. It is a true precursor to *The Dumb Waiter*.

Sources

Buck, R. A., "Pinter's *The Dumb Waiter*," in the *Explicator*, Vol. 56, No.1, Fall 1997, p. 45.

Burkman, Katherine H., *The Dramatic World of Harold Pinter: Its Basis in Ritual*, Ohio State University Press, 1971, p. 3.

Hinchliffe, Arnold P., *Harold Pinter*, Twayne Publishers, 1967, pp. 63, 68.

Hollis, James R., *Harold Pinter: The Poetics of Silence*, Southern Illinois University Press, 1970, pp. 43, 50.

Pinter, Harold, *The Dumb Waiter*, in *The Bedford Introduction to Drama*, edited by Lee A. Jacobus, St. Martin's Press, 1989, pp. 842-54.

Further Reading

Billington, Michael, *The Life and Work of Harold Pinter*, Faber and Faber, 1996.

> Billington combines biography and an examination of Pinter's works in the context of the events of his life.

Goodman, Paul, *Growing Up Absurd: Problems of Youth in the Organized System*, Random House, 1960.

> This book is a classic study of the effects of what Goodman calls "the organized society" that began to dominate the working and social lives of young people in the 1950s. *Growing Up Absurd* examines problems of powerlessness, meaninglessness, and capricious authority.

Kerr, Walter, *Harold Pinter*, Columbia University Press, 1967.

> A drama critic for the *New York Herald Tribune* and, after its collapse, for the *New York Times*, Kerr explores Pinter's plays as examples of existential suspense dramas.

Thompson, David T., *Pinter: The Player's Playwright*, Macmillan, 1985.

> Thompson examines the influence of Pinter's early and extensive career as an actor in repertory companies playing everything from classic Greek and Shakespearean dramas to Agatha Christie melodramas and his later career as a playwright.

Whyte, William H., *The Organization Man*, University of Pennsylvania Press, 2002

> Whyte's anatomy of 1950s corporate culture and its pervasive and coercive influence became a classic sociological study that defined much of the phenomena of that decade.